Daughter, You're Meant to Be YOU

Daughter, You're Meant to Be YOU

Living Elegantly by the Holy Spirit

Yvonne Sophia Low

ANGELSNDOVES

© 2024 Yvonne Sophia Low

Scripture marked (NKJV) taken from the New King James Version®. Copyright © 1982 by Thomas Nelson. Used by permission. All rights reserved.

Scripture quotations marked (KJV) are from The Authorized (King James) Version. Rights in the Authorized Version in the United Kingdom are vested in the Crown. Reproduced by permission of the Crown's patentee, Cambridge University Press.

Scripture quotations marked (NIV) are taken from the Holy Bible, New International Version®, NIV®. Copyright © 1973, 1978, 1984, 2011 by Biblica, Inc.™ Used by permission of Zondervan. All rights reserved worldwide. www.zondervan.com. The "NIV" and "New International Version" are trademarks registered in the United States Patent and Trademark Office by Biblica, Inc.™

Scripture quotations marked (ESV) are from the ESV® Bible (The Holy Bible, English Standard Version®), © 2001 by Crossway, a publishing ministry of Good News Publishers. Used by permission. All rights reserved. The ESV text may not be quoted in any publication made available to the public by a Creative Commons license. The ESV may not be translated in whole or in part into any other language.

Scripture quotations marked (NLT) are taken from the *Holy Bible*, New Living Translation, copyright ©1996, 2004, 2015 by Tyndale House Foundation. Used by permission of Tyndale House Publishers, Carol Stream, Illinois 60188. All rights reserved.

Cover illustration and design by Izabela Ciesinska

First published by ANGELSNDOVES 2024

Copyright © 2024 by Yvonne Sophia Low

All rights reserved. No part of this publication may be reproduced, stored or transmitted in any form or by any means, electronic, mechanical, photocopying, recording, scanning, or otherwise without written permission from the publisher. It is illegal to copy this book, post it to a website, or distribute it by any other means without permission.

Yvonne Sophia Low asserts the moral right to be identified as the author of this work.

First edition

ISBN: 978-981-18-9955-3 (Hardback)
ISBN: 978-981-18-9670-5 (Paperback)

First Printing, 2024

CONTENTS

DEDICATION viii

Preface 1

1 | Realizing your identity 3

2 | Come up higher 28

3 | When life and death are before you, choose LIFE 56

ABOUT THE AUTHOR 90

To you, beautiful daughter who holds this book.

May these words inspire you,

with love and blessings.

Preface

Prosperous life spans beyond material gain, it is the satisfaction of your soul that results in the outpouring of prosperity in every aspect of your life (3 John 1:2). How your life started is not nearly as important as how it will end. You may have had a harsh start with disadvantages due to the lack of opportunities, the lack of family resources to provide for you, the lack of a favorable environment, the lack of a good mentor to guide you, or some physical incapacity to perform. If you are willing to learn, to lean in, and to follow God's leading, you will come up higher and grow more bountifully than those who had it easy at the beginning.

But many who are first will be last, and the last first.
—Matthew 19:30, NKJV

In life there will be seasons of difficulties, but do not allow your heart to falter. Regardless of the number of bumps you encounter, the mistakes that you make, the injustice that is inflicted, none of these things can alter your destiny if you do not allow them to. Instead, shake off the difficulties each time they try to grab hold of you. Some seasons may be more difficult than others, and there might be many voices shouting at you and telling you blatantly to give up, but don't—only believe: He who had created you loves you and He has a plan for you (Jeremiah 29:11). Trust God. Through faith, wisdom, patience, and courage, you will eventually arrive where you were made to be, become all that you are meant to be, dignified and beautiful all around, in His grace.

It is my prayer that as you read through these pages, the Holy Spirit will guide you to understanding, show you His will for your life, and lead you to all truths in His peace, wholeness, and wellness.

Beloved, I pray that you may prosper in all things and be in health, just as your soul prospers. —3 John 1:2, NKJV

Yours sincerely,

Yvonne Sophia Low

Realizing your identity

I. *Mama's letter*

Beloved daughter,

Life might have put unexpected obstacles in your way, but you have been brave, and I'm very proud of you.

Surmounting hurdle after hurdle, you have persevered and done what you knew was best.

People around you have not been helpful; they have judged and criticized you and have caused you to doubt yourself and have a lower self-esteem. Numerous nights you have cried yourself to sleep with a deep void in your heart that felt like a dark, hollow bottomless pit.

You're weighed down by the tradition of a family

heritage in which the mediocre lives of others have engulfed you, oppressing all conceivable dreams you have. The truth of the matter is that no one knows your destiny better than your heavenly Father, who had it all planned (Jeremiah 29:11); your reality will only go as far as the imagination of your heart. Therefore guard your heart with all diligence, for out of it springs the issues of life (Proverbs 4:23).

The unpleasant circumstances of the past cannot deter you from your destiny. The deep desire in your heart, know that it was put there by God so that you will live it out to glorify His name. And He knows all about you and He loves you. You're precious in His eyes.

Love, Mama

II.   *Betsy*

Standing at the cross-junction, with people and cars thronging from all directions, Betsy felt lost and didn't know where to go. She stood hesitating, pondering over what had just struck her as reality—divorce proceedings had just begun with a petition made at the lawyer's office. On one hand, she was relieved over the soon-to-come release from the bondage of her husband, on the other hand, she was worried about how others would perceive her as a divorcee, especially her family—would they accept her back? Could she start her life all over again?

Betsy had been raised in a conservative family that was deeply rooted in its traditional customs. Girls were told to marry young and produce heirs for the family. They assumed the role of homemaker the moment they were married, and working in a professional job was rarely supported.

Four years ago, Betsy had left her family home and moved in with her husband. Life was simple with no expectations of anything extravagant. While on her façade Betsy looked contented, deep in her heart she yearned for more. Ever since her graduation from high school, she had wanted to pursue a professional degree to help her career advance up the corporate ladder, but no one in the family had encouraged it. Each time she had brought up the topic, she had experienced backlash.

Gradually, the desire had faded and she had stopped pursuing anything.

Betsy had always been obedient to her parents, and not once had she gone against them and defied their will. Her need to feel accepted and loved had paralyzed her and prevented her from pursuing her dreams. Her marriage, likewise, was the result of her dutifully obeying an order from her parents. She and her husband had been high school classmates, and they had started dating in their school days. When the parents had felt it was time for them to tie the knot, Betsy had conceded albeit having doubts in her heart. Just a year into the marriage, her husband began to beat her up whenever he was angry. By the end of the third year, the violence of her husband towards her became so bad that her nose broke during one of their fights and she had deep bruises all over her body. That day had been an awakening for her; she had decided she could take it no more and filed for a protection order against him.

Even though Betsy had been fortunate to survive the abuse, and now she could finally be free from her husband, she felt shame—the stigma of divorce, an almost unheard-of term in her family. Even as harm was inflicted, the women in the family would tolerate and live through it while pretending that everything was all right.

She stood at a crossroads, feeling apprehensive about her life. Tears began to roll down her cheeks. With her eyes shut, she stepped into the traffic.

III. Beyond tradition

By and large, family tradition and custom molds our lives, frames our beliefs, and influences the way we live. A child brought into a family learns by observing how others in the family behave and interact, absorbing all of that information and very quickly growing accustomed to those behaviors and interactions and making them her own.

Then, after several years of working in society and tuning in to the broader world, her perspective on things could evolve with the experiences and maturity of her persona or she could deny the change and choose to hang on to the traditions that she grew up with in her family. The latter choice is to a large extent the result of comfort and familiarity, as change requires effort and courage—from breaking out of the mold to being okay with uncertainty, and then doing and being something different, something outside the ordinary things that she has known and something that will help her realize her potential. Many people, even though they want change, have instead chosen to cling to the status quo and to what they have always known.

Abraham needed to move out of his father's land of idol worshippers before God could bless him. At seventy-five years of age, Abraham obeyed God and uprooted himself and his family to go to an unknown place, and the promises were fulfilled.

Our beliefs hold the key element that determines the destiny of our lives. Before we embark on the grandest mission of changing the world, it is important for us to understand that it is our belief system that propels our actions, resulting in where we end up. Whether we believe we have dignity and are made to live a blessed and fulfilling life, or whether we believe we are made to live a life of mediocrity and need to compromise our values in order to get ahead while following the path that has been shown to us, our beliefs essentially become the predominant force that shift our circumstances and cause change to take place.

IV.   Change your modus operandi

Thoughts and imagination

> *For as he thinketh in his heart, so is he.* —Proverbs 23:7, KJV

> *Cogito, ergo sum (I think, therefore I am).* —Rene Descartes

Your thoughts determine who you are; you're made up of the sum total of your thoughts, and soon enough your behavior will match them. That is, your thoughts shape your life, the imagination in your heart (Jeremiah 9:14).

Every innovation that we see in the world today is a result that originated as thoughts—first imagined and then manifested. For example, in the inventions of the airplane, the telephone, air-conditioning, and television in the nineteenth and twentieth centuries, and likewise in the continuous evolvement of technology in the current era and everything else that we are capable of imagining, there lies the possibility of seeing what we imagine come to pass. This shows that what we focus our thoughts and vision on can grow and eventually come about, for good or for evil.

Thoughts and imagination can also be manifested through words. Words that we use and think about ourselves, and words that people have said or written about us. By themselves, words don't reflect reality until we accept them. When we think about ourselves using words like "winner" and "loser," feelings are evoked that can cause those words to become our reality. When we start to internalize something, we are giving it credence and before long it begins to feel real. The unconscious process of our imagination is the fundamental influence of what may be—as Albert Einstein noted, imagination is greater than knowledge.

The good news is that the mind is not immutable. It is malleable and can be changed. Over the years, scientists have proven its versatility as we adapt ourselves conditionally—that is, we have absolute control over our minds by guarding what thoughts we allow to come into them.

Thoughts that are degrading and that serve no value to your growth are simply time wasters, so be quick to discard them and don't allow them to fester. When you are feeling unhappy or lousy over something that has happened, it's good to talk about it to someone you can trust or to pour out your thoughts and feelings to God, giving yourself the compassion to moan over what has happened but not to dwell on it. Then replace those thoughts and feelings by turning your mind to think of things that are good, energizing, and motivating, such as seeing your dreams come to pass and feeling the joy of it.

Gratitude is a good practice to fuel the mind. By remembering and appreciating all the good things and people you have been given, you begin to optimize your thoughts. In giving thanks, knowing it's all by grace that you have what you have, your heart broadens and softens, your eyes are enlightened, and you are ready to leap forth higher.

Write yourself a new story and alter your course

> *The only person you are destined to become is the person you decide to be.* —Ralph Waldo Emerson

To change your life, simply change your mind—the thoughts and imagination that have determined the choices and decisions that you have made for yourself—and your actions will follow.

Where we are in our lives right now is largely a result of decisions that we have made in the past that define who we are and what we do. These decisions include our job, the assets we own, the debts we have incurred, our hobbies, the people we have allowed into our inner circles, as well as the lifestyle we have adopted.

It doesn't matter what has transpired to put us in our current situation; if we don't like it we can change it, starting from our mind. Begin by imagining yourself in the future: What would you like to see? What steps do you need to take to make that happen? In reckoning this, it sometimes may feel overwhelming, but this is not about plotting out the entire journey—after all, no one can predict the unforeseeable in the future. Yet we should not be held ransom by the unpredictable. Instead, take one baby step of faith forward, celebrating one small victory at a time as we conquer each obstacle—more accurately, the obstacles of our own innate resistance.

Many times, people see obstacles as fate, and they think that it is their lot in life that they are predetermined not to have or be something. The truth of the matter is that obstacles are nothing more than roadblocks and we can choose to creatively and morally maneuver over them instead of being stopped by them. God wants only the best for us, and in Him there is nothing that is impossible to achieve. If there is something that you know He has put in your heart, seek Him to guide you towards it. The greatest obstacle is in fact the obstacle of the mind—the limiting mindset that we have in ourselves that is preventing us from moving forward and that goes back to our thoughts and imagination.

On the other hand, limitations such as scarce resources and opportunities can trigger the need to compete and push others down in order to get ahead. This is a typical mindset resulting from the fear of not having enough, of losing out to others. People with this limiting mindset see others as competitors, and they believe that the only way for them to rise up is to have others fall. It is a "me-win-you-lose" mentality that is self-centered and offers no value to anyone except the self. Such limitations prevent us from fulfilling our destiny, for His will for us is always to be a part of His greater work for the universe, and anything that diverges from His purpose is not of Him. Instead of looking at the limitations, what is far more important is to have the courage to live a life that is different from others—a life that you know is uniquely yours.

How we see ourselves dictates our future, and ultimately our beliefs reflect the life we live. While we are unable to change the past since it has already happened, we can certainly shift our future by making some changes, starting with ourselves. First accept what needs to change, then admit responsibility and act on it and change will happen. Then start acting like the person you want to become without allowing the present situation to interfere.

For where your treasure is, there your heart will be also.

—Matthew 6:21, Luke 12:34, NKJV

What is in your heart? What do you value and what are you passionate about? Therein lies your treasure. "Treasure" refers to our resources—practically, to our time and money. Where we spend our time and money is where our heart is, and our heart is what guides us in making the choices we make. To make better choices and decisions in life, check in with your heart and start making adjustments to how your resources should be spent. In short, if you don't want something in your future, don't give energy to it starting from now. Expend your resources only on what you want to see in your future, and your heart will go accordingly.

Look at your life right now, is there anything that is constantly causing you frustration? If yes, be glad because it is a sign signaling that change is needed. Whether you heed the need for change or ignore it boils down to how bad the frustration is. Think about how this issue, if left unchanged, will affect your future. Will it bring you closer to your desired self or further away? What do the consequences look like? How will these consequences make you feel if the issues are left unchanged? Oftentimes the issue can be resolved by making little changes in our habitual behavior, by replacing one actor with another and setting up a new narrative for ourselves.

Look at your lifestyle choices. For example, look at the daily use of your time—are you spending too much time on social media, critiquing and comparing with others? Look at the way you manage your money—are you spending money on items for the sake of proving something to others? Look at the friends you closely associate with—are the conversations and activities edifying? Look at your goals—is their purpose yours or someone else's? What are the motivations behind them? And look at the words you speak—do they glorify God? All of these choices become a reflection of yourself.

Then ask yourself these questions: Is my behavior and what I'm doing promoting virtues and virtuous beliefs such as having an abundant spirit and the belief that I'm more than enough? Is what I'm doing helping me to rise up higher and become who I truly am, created in God's likeness (Genesis 1:26)? Are my goals truly mine? Is what I'm doing bringing me closer to where I want to be? These questions may seem minuscule to the undiscerning eye, but the consequences they have for your future can possibly be the difference between success and failure.

Essentially your beliefs become your identity, and those beliefs guide your actions.

Figure: What you believe (belief) becomes who you are (identity), and who you are guide what you do (act).

V.   Who is she?

As she enters the room, the atmosphere instantly lights up. The impassive faces in the room turn upon seeing her and start showing color and warmth. A distinct aura is felt as she walks past each person, smiling and looking tenderly into their eyes. Everyone is drawn to her and wants to get close.

Have you ever experienced meeting someone like her, someone who instantly captivated you?

There is something about her that draws you in. She might be beautiful, but you know it is something deeper. Such is the aura that distinguishes her from the rest. The aura of confidence that is gentle and humble, yet self-assured. Who is she? you might ask.

What if she is you?

Your brand

How you carry yourself, your actions, your words, your attitude—these things show others who you are, and who you are becomes your brand that people resonate with. A brand of graciousness and elegance, or a brand of pride and small-mindedness? People remember you by what you show to them more than what you claim yourself to be. How you envision yourself should reflect in your brand. If you see yourself living in abundance, show the largeness of your heart to others by being gracious and giving.

Think for a moment about the brand Hermès: What comes to mind? Luxurious, exorbitance, exclusivity? Why? Because Hermès has been successful over the decades in marketing its brand as a top-notch label that appeals to the lavish lot who appreciate its luxury and exclusiveness, alongside its high price tag. It is intriguing to see that the company has remained strong and resilient over the years amid high competition. Hermès has retained its top spot owing to its brand that is familiar to its clients.

Similarly, your brand will go a long way, beyond the first impression that you create, as long as you are consistent in your actions and attitude. Essentially, the bigger you are on the inside, the greater you are on the outside, as John Maxwell, an American leadership guru, has rightly pointed out. So how would you like your brand to be remembered?

> *And we all, who with unveiled faces contemplate the Lord's glory, are being transformed into his image with ever-increasing glory, which comes from the Lord, who is the Spirit.* —2 Corinthians 3:18, NIV

VI.   Embrace and love thy art

> *"Art never expresses anything but itself."* —Oscar Wilde

Walking through an art gallery where dozens of artworks are put on display, you notice some pieces that beckon. They might not be considered to be in the category of excellence or be highly sought after, but for some reason they catch your eye. Your spirit connects with them. This is personal, not universal. Maybe they mean nothing to others. Maybe they only attract you.

You see many paintings. They are well-known—some are even famous and have won numerous accolades. You turn. That one, there, in the corner. You look away, but your eyes keep going back. You can't help yourself. You step closer—with careful tread as if afraid to break the silence. Your eyes are locked-in now. Time seems to freeze as you gaze at the painting's beauty. The other paintings—majestic and hued—do not call to you. This small one, this small white frame in the corner: it has connected with you.

Art is spiritual. The beauty of art is spiritual. When there's a connection between your spirit and the art, its beauty arises. You can see it. You can feel it. The emotion inside you bubbles up. This has no border; it has no limit. It knows no convention but to respond to the inner desire that springs forth from the soul. And that is beautiful, as acclaimed by the legendary Russian painter and art theorist, Wassily Kandinsky. Neither benchmark nor validation is required. You are just attracted to it. Even if the famous painting *Mona Lisa*, a masterpiece of renowned artist Leonardo Da Vinci that is famous as one of the most beautiful works ever created, is hanging beside it. You are pleased—very pleased—gratified by the beauty of the art in your hand.

> *To love oneself is the beginning of a lifelong romance.* —Oscar Wilde

And you, my daughter, are your Daddy God's master art piece. Carefully and delicately wrought by Him, He sees that you are beautiful like none other. Unique and precious, you transcend beyond the conventional definition of beauty and more. Look to Him, for His love for you never fails.

Romanticized loving relationships are elusive, like grasping wind in your hands, and even illusory, like beginning to see wings and a crown on a swine.

They are not even reliable, instead they wobble like small boats in the vast ocean. There is always a nagging feeling that you want more—the longing to be loved and cherished as much as you have hope for the relationship. Only to have it all fall apart as soon as the partner gets what he wants, like when the honeycomb reaches the lips and melts away. And you wonder, is this all that there is?

Maybe you've given in too soon. Maybe you've misunderstood. And maybe . . . maybe you just don't need it at all. Since the world is now a place where films and productions are commonplace, the dreamy eros between men and women that is portrayed in these stories has started gripping our hearts and minds, stirring an intense yearning inside us—a force that is immaterial yet powerful enough to cause a torpedo capable of destroying what's meant to be beautiful when in its most utterly pure form. Does true love even exist? you ask.

My daughter, look away from all these erroneous pictures of love and begin to love yourself. This is not lofty or self-aggrandizing. For you've been created with precious stones and a foundation of sapphire (Isaiah 54:11). You're priceless. The thieves would come to steal, so be vigilant by valuing yourself.

When you were just a thought, an imagination of being, an

art piece without a border, you were a spirit with a beautiful narrative yet to emerge. Then you came into existence when your form was created.

You are not serendipitous but a premeditated creation by your great artist, God the Father, who holds your beginning and end in His hands. And He knows all about you and loves you.

You are precious, valuable—if only you knew! Your love journey begins in reckoning His love for you—an amazing, one-of-a-kind love that nothing can supplant. In His abundance, you are filled and more—you cannot contain His love so it overflows to those around you. You can love because you have first received love from Him and your romance begins within. The same way a car can't drive if it has an empty tank, you can't love if you have an empty heart without feeling worn out, yet mortal man cannot fill your empty heart.

This is where your lifelong romance begins. His love gives you the confidence to pursue life, to give and to receive. In His love, there's no fear, neither do you have to fend for yourself. And as He provides for the bird in the air, think about how much more He will give to you, His beloved.

> *"Though the mountains be shaken*
> *and the hills be removed,*
> *yet my unfailing love for you will not be shaken*
> *nor my covenant of peace be removed,"*
> *says the LORD*
> —Isaiah 54:10, NIV

Take pride in your gifts

Do you know that you're a gift from God, and that various gifts have been given to you? From the day you were born you were given a destiny to fulfill, a destiny of your joy and to benefit others, a destiny to complete a part of His jigsaw puzzle in His grandiose plan on earth, and a destiny that will bring you the greatest satisfaction if you embrace it. You were made for this. Unless you pigheadedly refuse to accept, it will not go away, for it was ordained for a reason and you were chosen for it.

Your destiny is fit for God's purpose at His time, with the use of your gifts, and your role evolves through the passage of time.

Your confidence increases each time you use your gifts to accomplish your role; you will experience a flow that is so supernaturally natural that you will know you're on the right path. Take pride in the gifts that God has given you as He takes pride in you. Even if you feel they are mediocre, they are yours, unique and without compare. They are a sign of His love for you, and you can acknowledge Him by using your gifts in pride and by depending solely on His goodness. And God will use your gifts to bless you in ways that exceed your expectations.

Your mystery is alluring

> *The most beautiful experience we can have is the mysterious. It is the fundamental emotion that stands at the cradle of true art and true science.*
> —Albert Einstein

Anything that arouses curiosity is beautiful. The more mysterious and mystical it is, the scarcer and more exquisitely valuable it becomes, and the more it causes men to intensely desire it and to go crazy trying to find it and possess it. Like a super luxurious car that is labeled with a hefty price tag, coveted by many yet accessible only to the enviable few.

As a propellant ignites an explosive charge in a gun, so does a mysterious and valuable person or object kindle a fire of desire to erupt in men. A man would dig, stalk, sneak, plot, chase, dream, climb the mountain, scale the avalanche, swim the torrent, and fight the boar just to get close to his object of desire. Even for a small encounter, a glimpse of its beauty, it's all worth it. The brief encounter or glimpse is sufficient to satisfy the primal craving within himself until he wants it more. The man will not give up. Not until you give it away, too soon, too fast.

Daughter, do you know you are created mysteriously? Your personality, your thoughts, your passion, your eloquence, your femininity, and your body—it's all so uniquely crafted. Nobody is constructed in the exact same way as you, and nobody can be. Though a copycat may imitate you and try to sound like you, they are far from being you.

Your passion is beautifully presented in your works, which make others want to know you more. Your femininity is a strong asset that has the power to melt a hardened heart (Proverbs 25:15), the strength to heal divisions, and the wisdom to build up a house (Proverbs 14:1; see also Proverbs 24:3-4). And your body, oh so mystically formed, has the capability to bring forth life.

Your boundary, the non-negotiable limits, the personal space are sacred between you and God, so guard them zealously. Be bold to make known to others your values, priorities, and what you can't do and can't accept, and stand your ground. People who value and love you will respect you for who you are, and you will be more in harmony with yourself the more you value your boundary. Your self-respect in owning your boundary and not giving in to compromise makes you far from being a people-pleaser, but instead makes you a God-pleaser and that alone is beautiful. That same self-respect strengthens your confidence in living out your identity and undertaking projects that reflect you, exuding the spirit of the love of life. People are drawn to you not merely on a surface level but by a deeper attraction, and they desire to be in your presence.

The man can only imagine. His mind wanders and seeks every day to come close. When he comes, consider what is before you—a knife to your throat if you give in to his sweet sayings. Do not desire his words, for they are deceptive (Proverbs 23:1–3). But be satisfied in your soul in God your perfect love, that you will loathe the honeycomb planted in your way (Proverbs 27:7).

> You are precious my daughter, and when you respect yourself, your body, your being, and what you have been given, you will be honored.

Come up higher

I. Mama's letter

Beloved daughter,

I know you've been diligent in your work, and have completed all the tasks that were assigned to you, but somehow there's this constant dissatisfaction tugging at your heart. You hope for a more interesting life and have tried pursuing things that you thought might make a difference but nothing has really been gratifying. You have wanted to venture out, but you were too afraid of failure and that people might mock you. You often seek distraction by indulging in short-term pleasure, only to find yourself feeling empty. You live life from day to day, seemingly with no real purpose to look forward to. Often you find yourself comparing yourself to others, which inadvertently makes you feel dejected. You have entrusted your hope to a person you thought you could rely on only to end up with disappointment.

Daughter, your heavenly Father has a great plan for your life. The dissatisfaction you've been experiencing is a sign that you're meant for something bigger and larger than yourself. When you were created, special talents and gifts were given to you, and it is for you to find them and use them for His glory. He will put desires in your heart if you will seek Him, and He will work alongside you to see them to fruition. You may go through trials and tribulations but do not be afraid, for He has given you the grace and strength needed to combat them.

Father God loves you very much, and His desire is to see you grow and become all that you can be. Your growth and every step you take along the way are what signifies success. Life is a journey, a continuous learning trek. As you lean on God and abide in Him, He will cause your steps to be prosperous, which will bring about the enlargement of your heart and your capacity to receive and to give. Ultimately you were created for the larger purpose of His vision, and only by fulfilling your call in Him will you be truly gratified, having experience unparalleled exponential joy.

Love, Mama

II.   *Cinder*

Cinder came home one evening and found an envelope that someone had slid under her door. She picked it up and was surprised to see the words "To My Love" written on the front of the envelope. Now Cinder had been single for a decade since the passing of her fiancé. Though she had male friends that she hung out with, she didn't consider any of them suitable for a relationship. Over the years, some of them had turned out to be weeds that caused frustration, but God had been quick to pluck them out before Cinder's life became disrupted.

Cinder opened up the envelope and found a nicely folded letter filled with modern calligraphic writing. It was filled with memories about France and the good times shared between the sender and the recipient. The letter was well written, but there was no mention of the sender's or the intended recipient's names. Neither was there a postage stamp affixed.

Obviously it's a prank, Cinder thought, a neighbor must have played a trick on her. She had never been to France, though for a long time it had been her dream to visit the country with her husband one day.

But how she enjoyed reading the love letter, which had her

mesmerized. She couldn't help admiring the beautiful writing. Fond memories of the past began to flood her mind.

The sweetness of her late fiancé, Bob, and the good times they had shared were so vivid that it felt as if it had all just happened yesterday. On his bed in the intensive care unit, Bob had breathed his last breath and passed on, and Cinder had collapsed. No one had expected her to survive through the ordeal knowing how heartbroken she was. They had just renovated their home, and it was only a few months to their wedding when suddenly Bob fell ill. He was sent to the hospital and was diagnosed with lymphoma cancer. Immediately he was put on intensive treatment. However, in just a short period of time, complications began to occur and it became apparent that the cancer and the complications were too much for his body to take and so it started to crash.

Shortly after his passing, Cinder went home one day after church with an intense emptiness in her heart. As the pain and sorrow inside her began to swell up, Cinder knew she could take it no longer. She began to gobble up all the sleeping pills she could find and downed them with alcohol. Soon her mind slipped into unconsciousness. Then she saw herself in a bright cloud overlooking huge plots of land. Her body felt light and there was an overflowing joy springing forth from within her that she had never experienced before.

Suddenly she woke up and found a strong energy gushing inside her. She felt so alive and didn't know what had just happened, if that had been an out-of-the-body experience, but she knew it was God. She felt that God had given her a new life. In the following days, she began to see hope and a new vision for herself.

Gradually, Cinder began to thrive in her undertakings and to achieve the goals she had set for herself. God had blessed her with so much, more than what she had ever imagined when she was with Bob. Her life was totally transformed, and she never looked back.

III. *Fix the bulb, no sweat*

"Oops, it's blown out!" Just the other day, when I was having dinner on the balcony, the ceiling light started to flicker before it went bust. I took a ladder and climbed up to the ceiling to check. This proved to be harder than expected, for the lamp holder was so intricately made that finding the opening was a challenge. I knew I could easily outsource the job to an expert, but I thought I should first evaluate the situation before I decided what to do. After about fifteen minutes of navigation, I was still unable to pry open the holder and my neck had become sore. At that moment, giving up would seem like a logical response, but something inside me was unwilling to let go. I took a deep breath and continue to work on the situation. After another thirty minutes, I finally found the opening and was able to remove the faulty bulb. The next day, I bought a new bulb and inserted it into the holder. When the light came back on again, I was so delighted because an unexpected goal had been accomplished.

> *A desire accomplished is sweet to the soul.*
> —Proverbs 13:19, NKJV

Do the hard thing

> And He said to me, "My grace is sufficient for you, for My strength is made perfect in weakness."
> —2 Corinthians 12:9, NKJV

When we first embark on something new, inevitably we feel uncomfortable and ill-equipped. To dismiss the new goal and convince ourselves that it's not our thing may seem like an easy way out, but instead it gives root to a self-defeating mindset that reappears whenever something hard comes up in our lives. We learn while working with our hands and it gets easier as time goes on. Even though the unfamiliar may seem intimidating at first, momentum begins to flow if we do not give up.

We won't know our true potential until we begin to push the limits that we have unconsciously put upon ourselves. When we leave the familiar and expand our limits, a new growth pattern emerges in us, forming a higher limit and increasing our tolerance threshold. And each time we push our limits, our tolerance threshold is stretched and the task before us becomes easier. Often it is the hard things we experience that prepare us for bigger things in life, the opportunities that God is bringing us.

Rahab in the Bible was a foreigner and a woman of ill repute, but she trusted God and had the courage to hide the Israelite spies despite the threat of death to both herself and her family from her city's authorities. She did it by faith after hearing all the amazing works that God had done for His people (Joshua 2:9–11). As a result, her life story was rewritten and she became the ancestor of King David, and her name is included in the genealogy of our Lord Jesus Christ.

During World War II, women were called to step out of their homes and help in the war industry by doing hard labor work, which was unacceptable in society prior to the war. That experience totally disrupted women's then presumed duty of tending to their children and households, and they were able to break away from their previous expectations and limitations and transform their lives.

Most girls in their teenage years spend their school vacations enjoying themselves, but Cinder would find a part-time job in order to make some money. Though the jobs were menial and often tough work, Cinder had learned to persevere. That same resilience had given her the strength to bounce back during the difficult times of her life and to thrive while treading her path and achieving her goals.

They were prepared—Rahab, the women during the time of World War II, Cinder, and the many others who have gone through hardships and challenging situations in their lives and later achieved breakthroughs. No one likes suffering, but the truth of the matter is that it's only through the difficult times that we learn and grow in our character if we will not give up. For suffering produces endurance and patience, which in turn produces character and brings us hope, and such hope does not disappoint, delude, or shame us (Romans 5:3–5).

When we are enjoying ourselves, it is rare that anything useful can be learned beyond our enjoyment of life. It is the unprecedented situations and the challenging moments of our lives that shift our perspectives and launching us into new territories with new limits. And by faith we walk through it all and come up stronger. If we know that God operates by faith before things begin to move, then when we take steps of faith, trusting Him even when we don't see anything, our faith is strengthened and our confidence grows as a result. Sometimes the hard season may be longer than expected, but we can have full confidence that we are coming into a new beautiful season and are prepared for it. The greater the harvest that is ahead of you, the more preparation is needed so that at the right time and the right place all things come together perfectly.

> *But let patience have its perfect work, that you may be perfect and complete, lacking nothing.*
> —James 1:4, NKJV

Let go, don't look back

> *Brothers, I do not consider that I have made it my own. But one thing I do: forgetting what lies behind.* —Philippians 3: 13, ESV

Somehow holding onto the familiar past gives comfort, even if that past contains chains of events that brought more pain than joy. It's the certainty that people crave. This holding on, unfortunately, creates resistance within ourselves and makes breakthroughs difficult to achieve. Like driving a car forward when our focus is on the rearview mirror, it is unlikely that we will reach our destination.

When we look back, we are burdened by the weight of the past, and memories of the hurt and pain that we experienced are evoked. We inevitably beat ourselves up, which consumes time and energy that could otherwise be used for creative pursuits. The mind cannot operate at its optimum capacity with the negative energy from those memories flowing at the same time. The book of James says, "out of the same mouth proceed blessing and cursing" (James 3:10, NKJV), and goes on to say that this should not happen. It is detrimental to our very being.

We obtain a new perspective when we let go of the past that

previously dominated our mind and vision. The fog vanishes as we release our grip, and then we are able to see things more clearly and make new and wiser decisions. By holding onto the past, we allow it to continue affecting our life as we relive the bad experiences, so much so that the blessings before us in the present become unrecognizable. Often people lament about the unfairness and lack of blessings in their lives, and their resistance to positive change and blessings becomes clear to them only when they decisively learn to let go, to forgive, and to dismiss the past.

When we forgive, the heaviness that previously weighed on us begins to diminish. Realizing that people might not have known better when they acted and that all of us are works in progress and journeying as we grow gives us the compassion to forgive, and that includes the forgiveness of ourselves for the mistake that we have made.

Forgiving is an acceptance of what has happened, and it leads to peace. While we may not approve of what has been done, we can release the hold it had on our minds and free ourselves to live more authentically in the present. It's an ongoing process as we learn to let go. Unpleasant memories will come up from time to time, but we can choose to let them pass and redirect our focus instead of trying to fight against them.

Sometimes, while en route to our destiny, memories of past achievements may also pose hindrances to our undertakings.

When things in the present do not seem to be where we think they should be, we start to feel shortchanged. We need to remember, however, that life is never linear but instead consists of different opportunities and experiences as we grow, and each of these opportunities and experiences are unique, which makes comparison unnecessary. Instead of allowing our expectations to affect our emotions, let's learn to embrace the present and flow with it in trust and openness, and we will begin to find a greater appreciation of life.

The present is a gift, and peace and serenity flow out from within when we consciously choose to focus on the present. We find harmony with ourselves when we live untethered from the attachment of the past and from thoughts of the future.

Humility to serve

> *But he who is greatest among you shall be your servant.* —Matthew 23:11, NKJV

> *The reward of humility and the fear of the Lord is riches and honor and life.* —Proverbs 22:4, ESV

Serving others does not make one less than; in fact, it demonstrates the quintessential humanity of who we are in fulfilling our larger purpose in God. "As each has received a gift, use it to serve one another, as good stewards of God's varied grace" (1 Peter 4:10, ESV). Humility to serve is attractive; it makes us look more attractive than we already are. Contrary to what many may think, you stand out when you serve humbly unto the Lord.

The willingness to put others before ourselves, to think of others' needs and to respect them for who they are, are all traits of humility that are precious in God's eyes. For sure it is not always easy, especially if the other parties are rude and condescending towards us. In those times we have to remind ourselves of our true identity in God as His precious beloved, and that we are secure in Him regardless of how people behave towards us. Remember that when we serve it's not about the location, the capacity, or the people around us, but about God whom we ultimately serve. By surrendering to God, we see Jesus in spite of the flaws of others, and what seems impossible in without God becomes possible.

It is not coincidence that when one is humble, many other great attributes, such as compassion, kindness, gentleness, and patience, are demonstrated. Somehow the spirit of humility triggers similar positive traits. It is very unlikely for someone with a haughty spirit to display these traits in a genuine fashion. Only when our spirit is transformed from haughtiness to humility are others likely to gravitate to us, and without that transformation it is even impossible for us to serve in a way that benefits others.

IV.   Go Big

Single-mindedness

> *Therefore, my beloved brethren, be steadfast, immovable, always abounding in the work of the Lord, knowing that your labor is not in vain in the Lord.* —1 Corinthians 15:58, NKJV

> *A double minded man is unstable in all his ways.* —James 1:8, KJV

In the world we live in today, distraction is ubiquitous. Voices everywhere are trying to get our attention, drawing us to listen and to follow them. Even when something was never in our agenda, it suddenly becomes our thing to do as we see the people around us adopting it. If we do not have strong minds and strong convictions, and if we do not know what we stand for and what we believe in, we will inevitably fall into and be deceived by the worldviews and agendas presented by the voices around us.

Imagine setting a goal at the beginning of the year and then getting sidetracked. This doesn't happen because of a lack of time and resources, it happens because of a lack of conviction and focus. The desire to see the goal come to pass wasn't strong enough to follow through in the midst of distractions and other life events. This is the same reason why a huge number of people in recent years are experiencing anxiety and depression, which results in many taking compromising paths that lead to more pain.

Focus is key. Stay single-minded in our beliefs, which form the trajectory of our lives and direct us in the decisions we make.

There are times when situations are tough and pain and struggle afflict us, but if we continue to stay single-minded and follow God, distraction and contrary voices cannot distract us from our call. Neither can the dark forces that seek to oppress our minds, as they will have no room to fester.

We may not understand what's going on around us; the odds might be against us; we may be waiting for a turnaround that is not forthcoming; things might seem to be getting worse; and we might feel helpless and wonder if anything at all is going to change. Don't give up, my daughter. Press on and dig your heels in. Stand your ground and trust God. In the darkest hour, there is light on the horizon. Your dawn is coming. Your breakthrough is just around the corner. It is near, for your next stop is filled with abundance. You are set to be catapulted to the next level. Be steadfast.

We went through fire and through water; But You brought us out to rich fulfillment. —Psalm 66:12, NKJV

The truth of the matter is, God responds to faith. "According to your faith let it be to you" (Matthew 9:29, NKJV). Why did Caleb inherit the Promised Land while others died without entering? It was His faith; he was convicted and believed that God would keep His promises. So he remained steadfast in God even when everyone else was wavering with their unbelief and engaging in sinful activities.

Another faith picture is Joseph's story, which is a timeless classic. Of all stories about rags-to-riches, this is cream of the crop. More than a description of arising to great success from nothing, this story paints a picture of strong faith. Faith that allowed Joseph to withstand failure after failure and the injustices and suffering that befell him. Eventually Joseph was brought to triumph, and he stood tall before his enemies and became the most powerful man of Egypt, second only to Pharaoh in the ancient history.

Genesis 39:2 says, "The LORD was with Joseph, and he was a successful man" (NKJV). God called him a successful man even when it seemed unlikely, as Joseph was still a slave with nothing on his back. Only God knows the future of each person. He calls forth in the present what one will and should be. It was God's presence in Joseph's life that made him successful, and it was only a matter of time until what was seen in the natural circumstance began to shift and God's glory was manifested through Joseph. God's presence refers to a consciousness of Him and His promises. It was repeated a few times in Genesis that God was with Joseph, like in Genesis 39:23 when it says, "because the LORD was with him; and whatever he did, the LORD made it prosper" (NKJV).

Likewise for you, my daughter, know that God is with you today and always, and you are already a successful lady. Be conscious of God and His promises. It doesn't matter what you see or don't see in the natural circumstances around you, and what you have or don't have now, because God is with you and His presence in your life is what that makes you successful. At the right time, His glory shall be manifested through you in your life. Only believe, and never compromise and act like the world tells people they need to act in order to get ahead in life. That route will only lead to grief. Know that when God blesses, no sorrow shall be added (Proverbs 10:22). Never be motivated by fear. Wait on Him.

Be bold and courageous

> *Obstacles cannot crush me. Every obstacle yields to stern resolve. He who is fixed [on God] does not change his mind.* —Leonardo da Vinci, slight alteration mine

> *Watch, stand fast in the faith, be brave, be strong.* —1 Corinthians 16:13, NKJV

"It's about how hard you can get hit and keep moving forward. How much you can take and keep moving forward. That's how winning is done!" This is line from a speech in the movie *Rocky*, a three-time Oscar award-winning film. As a matter of fact, nobody is going to roll out a red carpet for you just because you have decided to pursue a dream. Instead, you will likely encounter challenges and people who do not believe in you. But be persistent and continue to run your course, not allowing any adversary to get you down even when nothing seems to be going right. You can reroute your plan, but never give up on a dream that you know God has instilled in you, however long it takes.

The male lead of the movie, Rocky, played by Sylvester Stallone, was a real-life Rocky himself who had battered through hardships and eventually reached the top. Stallone was born paralyzed in the lower left part of his face, but he was not deterred and wanted to become an actor. He went on to pursue his acting career in New York, but he was faced with one closed door after another. At the lowest point of his life, he was so broke that he had to sleep at a bus terminal for three weeks. He could not afford to feed both himself and his only buddy, his dog, anymore, so he had to sell his dog for a mere twenty-five dollars in order to feed himself. When he finally got the idea to put together the script that later became the film *Rocky* and was offered a handsome sum for it, he pushed back and negotiated to act in the film as the main character instead. The producer refused, not seeing his potential, but Stallone persisted and was willing to take only a small fraction of the sum offered, just enough for him to get by. He was at a great disadvantage when the deal was made, as he had no medical coverage and no aid was given to him when he suffered from the multiple injuries he incurred while acting in the role. His perseverance finally paid off, however, when the film hit the global box office and turned Stallone into a renowned celebrity.

Now, we don't have to get bashed up and suffer injuries like Stallone did in order to achieve our dreams. Stallone's story was used as an illustration of a man who would fight at all costs to fulfill his dream. For us, we have Jesus. If a dream is given to us by Him, He will guide and lead us through, and at the right and opportune time it shall come to pass. We need to only fix our eyes on Him and run our course, be undeterred by our circumstances. Of course, it is often said that things are easier said than done. In reality, there will be sacrifices that we need to make and certain things that we need to give up, but know that these are usually material things and it's for a finite period that we give them up. God will bring us to a new higher level with greater things when we come into our new season. However, know that God will never ask us to give up our family, health, or values. In fact, the material sacrifices are part of the plan to grow our character, to make us stronger in persevering towards who and what we want to become. With fewer material things, there are also fewer distractions, making it possible for us to be fully present in following our call.

It is true that when your desire to achieve your dream surpasses your fear of what you will lose, you are enroute to your success. Again, "what you will lose" refers to the material sacrifices and adjustments that we are willing to make in order to get to where we want to be. We need to make room for new and better things, and for that to happen, some other things need to be cut out.

While on our journey, we are bound to face difficulties, they are just part and parcel of life. Though we can't always control what happens to us or our circumstances, we can always decide how we want to respond to each situation. As Viktor Frankl, an Austrian neurologist, psychiatrist, and Holocaust survivor said: "Between stimulus and response there is a space. In that space is our power to choose our response. In our response lies our growth and our freedom." How we respond to a situation shows our stage of growth in life and that indicates how much farther we need to go to reach our destiny.

When we suffer from disadvantages, challenges, or closed doors while pursuing our call, it would be easy to just give up, but in doing so we would become stuck, limiting our growth, and we would end up encountering the same obstacles again and again. Only when we learn how to cope and, in spite of our setbacks, to continue with our pursuits do we break through them and move up higher to a new level. Sometimes a closed door may not necessarily be a bad thing, as it can be a sign of God's protection over us. Only He knows if something is right for us and if it'll bring us pain. Allow God to lead and direct you and trust that if a door is closed, He will open another door for you that suits you better and brings you joy.

God has not promised us a bed of roses in life, but He did promise that we can have peace in Him, for He overcome the world for us (John 16:33). It is when we shift our focus from God to the world that we become fearful and discouraged. Peter was able to walk on water when he put his focus on Jesus, but the moment he shifted his focus to the storm, he sank (Matthew 14:29–30).

For our light affliction, which is but for a moment, is working for us a far more exceeding and eternal weight of glory, while we do not look at the things which are seen, but at the things which are not seen. For the things which are seen are temporary, but the things which are not seen are eternal. —2 Corinthians 4:17–18, NKJV

Often God uses circumstances to stretch our faith, for it is faith that pleases Him (Hebrews 11:6). Though rarely to our liking, it is the tough seasons of our lives that allow our character to grow. It is like being polished by sandpaper to remove our hard edges. Know that whatever call God has given to us, His ultimate objective is to see us grow in our character and be transformed more and more into His likeness, which will help us in fulfilling our destiny.

We know an adolescent has become an adult not by her age but by her actions—that is, when she stops pushing blame on others when bad things happen and instead takes responsibility to change or address the situation and then moves on without dwelling on it; when she starts to live in her call, unencumbered by the things and people around her; when she steps out to live according to her values regardless of others' approval; when she single-mindedly runs her course, pursuing what God has put in her heart even when nothing in the world around her makes sense. It is when she knows who she is in Christ and that God loves her that she will live out her identity, aligning her actions with her faith.

Our spiritual growth is all that matters as we progress in our call, for our soul's prosperity is the source of all blessings in our lives. That is, your call in life exists to help you become all that God has created you to be. It is a journey of faith, but be bold and courageous for the journey is meant to promote you and bring you closer to God. Trust what God has put in your heart and run with it. Do not give up, for He has your back.

Enlarge your tent

> *The Lord your God will soon bring you into the land He swore to give you when He made a vow to your ancestors Abraham, Isaac, and Jacob. It is a land with large, prosperous cities that you did not build. The houses will be richly stocked with goods you did not produce. You will draw water from cisterns you did not dig, and you will eat from vineyards and olive trees you did not plant.* —Deuteronomy 6:10–11, NLT

Rejoice and break forth into singing, my daughter! For now is the time when God is doing a new thing and bringing you into a new season of your life!

Get ready for it. Enlarge your faith and expand your vision. Get past your pain and make way for what God has put in your heart.

Learn that new skill, new language, new instrument, or new sport that you have always admired. Start imagining how you will feel when you learn it and are successful at it. Linger on those thoughts of joy and gladness and begin to make plans for learning the skill and try them out. Stretch your limits and be confident in your abilities.

Your horizons and perspectives will be broadened as you work on the new skill, and your capacities will be increased, raising you to a new level. As you enter the new territory, more new opportunities will open up for you. Do not be complacent, keep learning and growing, and stay steadfast to what is in your heart. If it is something that God has called you to, it will not dwindle.

When something seems too big for us to accomplish in the natural world, know that God is bigger than the whole universe put together and He has you in the palm of His hand (Psalm 24:1–2). In other words, He is in control and He is closely keeping watch over and safeguarding His beloved—you! Therefore, trust Him and focus on His greatness to help you succeed. He will equip you and give you the grace to work on your call when you commit it all unto Him.

As you go about following your call and working on your goal, know that the devil will constantly be attempting to disturb you and steal your peace. Be therefore vigilant and aware of the devil's plot so as not to give in to temptation. Guard your heart and mind by focusing on God through prayer and His words. Keep on keeping on, firing up on your work relentlessly. Do not give time to disturbances but trust God to make it all good for you.

Put on the whole armor of God, that you may be able to stand against the wiles of the devil. . . . Above all, taking the shield of faith with which you will be able to quench all the fiery darts of the wicked one. And take the helmet of salvation, and the sword of the Spirit, which is the word of God; praying always with all prayer and supplication in the Spirit, being watchful to this end with all perseverance and supplication for all the saints. —Ephesians 6:11, 6:16–18, NKJV

Though we may not know what the future holds, we can have confidence in God and always have the expectation that good things will come to us even when we don't yet see the manifestation of our desires fulfilled in our lives. God works in mysterious ways and His way is higher than ours (Isaiah 55:9). We first receive in the spiritual realm and then the physical, and everything in between happens through faith before we see the manifestation occur. "But without faith it is impossible to please Him, for he who comes to God must believe that He is, and that He is a rewarder of those who diligently seek Him" (Hebrews 11:6, NKJV).

Ultimately God's plan for us is to prosper us, to give us hope and a future (Jeremiah 29:11). And with certainty God is calling you, my daughter, into a big life, a life larger than yourself, a life that holds blessings and joy that you have not yet known. Your soul will be so enraptured and filled that you will not want anything else. Years later when you think back, all your present needs will suddenly become so minute in comparison to what you have received.

You shall remember and feel your past failures and pain no more. Where there's injustice done to you, God shall recompense. The pain inflicted on you will become such a distant memory that it will be as if it had never happened, for God is going to reverse it. He is going to rebuild, restore, and renew you (Isaiah 61).

Do not fear, for you will not be ashamed; neither be disgraced, for you will not be put to shame; for you will forget the shame of your youth. —Isaiah 54:4, NKJV

You will rise up with a glorious new identity, and people who knew you in the past will not recognize you, for God is doing a great thing for you and through you.

As you wholly follow God, He shall adorn you with many beautiful things and days, and with peace and gladness that will spring forth from the depths of your soul (Isaiah 54:11–14).

People will be drawn to you by your spirit, and your impact shall linger through generations.

God will vindicate you for the wrongs done to you and will bless you with victory, and He will give credence to your work and you shall receive honor. You will stand tall in His righteousness and be beautified so that He is glorified (Isaiah 61:3).

> *Make ready for God's blessing, you who are pining and groaning for greater things than these; God is about to bless you. Enlarge your tents; lengthen the*

cords, and strengthen the stakes; prepare for the coming blessing, for you are to have better and brighter days than you have ever yet known. Therefore be no more sad, but look forward with joyful anticipation to the good things in store for you. —Charles Spurgeon

When life and death are before you, choose LIFE

I. Mama's letter

Beloved daughter,

Of all things that you pursue, I urge you to pursue wisdom and make it your primary pursuit always. For therein lies life, and life more abundantly, without which all merited titles and accomplishments will come to naught as a ring of gold in a swine's snout or a beautiful woman without discretion. You are not that, as you have been given the spirit of discernment. You are able to live free and untethered as you make wisdom your guardian, pursuing it relentlessly by seeking the Lord.

Your ways will be pleasant and you'll know how to steer your course and lead others to truth. You'll be able to see beyond the surface and to make the right decisions with clarity even when evil attempts to manipulate your heart. Wisdom is your shield and your hidden treasure that will guard your life so that you won't be enticed by sinners. You'll walk steadfastly and you won't be greedy for gain. You'll live securely without fear.

When you receive wisdom, you receive the knowledge of God and find favor and high esteem in the sight of God and man. Wisdom will present you with a crown of beauty and glory, and your path shall be like the light of dawn that shines brighter and brighter until the perfect day.

Wisdom gives you the lips to speak words that feed, guide, and heal many and the understanding to know when it's time to keep mum. Your house is built and all the rooms are filled (Proverbs 24:3–4), and you shall flourish and yield rich fruits.

Wisdom will teach you to guard your heart with diligence and not to give your power away by paying attention to insults and people who steal your peace. She will also give you knowledge about men, whom you should and should not associate with, and she will show to you the right kind of man to marry.

With wisdom you're assured of a future and a reward, and your hope and expectation will not be cut off.

These promises are for you, my daughter, the righteous one in Christ Jesus. And the victory of His Resurrection is living in you. Walk in it.

Love, Mama

II.   Amy

"I thereby pronounce you guilty of frauds committed as managing director of Amy Investment Private Limited. . . . You are sentenced to two years of imprisonment and a fine of $500,000, as you are in violation of Companies Act sections . . ." Tears began to flood Amy's eyes when the judge passed the sentence. She looked down at her shoulder, feeling disgraced and ashamed. Her worst nightmare had come true. She sat in the defendant's seat looking hopeless. Her mind went blank while waiting to be ushered out.

The last few months had been rough, and not only was Amy struggling with the repetitive interrogations from the commercial investigation officers, she was also a nervous wreck over the sudden dissolution of her marriage. She could neither eat nor sleep, her heart was full of anxiety, and she could not fathom what had happened. She had thought her business was running well and her marriage was flourishing, only to find out later that it was all a hoax.

Even after she was told of the criminal suit against her business, she continued to go to work and tried to pretend like nothing had happened, but she was soon knocked back into reality by the investigations.

Remorse and dejection filled her heart as she looked back

on her life. How she wished she could turn back the clock and make better decisions this time.

Amy had been born with a silver spoon in her mouth and lacked for nothing in her life. Her friends generally saw her as someone who had it all together. Her parents had inherited a thriving family business and they gave Amy, their only child, everything she wanted. At the same time, they were very protective of her, setting up schedules and plans and making all decisions for her. That had, unfortunately, rendered her incapable of making good decisions on her own.

During her university years abroad, Amy had fallen into bad company, had picked up alcohol, cigarettes, and drugs, and was out partying every weekend. She met a boy and they started dating and became intimate and then she got pregnant. She did not tell her parents about it but went and aborted the baby herself. Her relationship with the boy then ended. In her graduating year, her friends asked her to partner with them in a business. Though she had no experience or knowledge of the business structure, she said yes to them to stay in their favor, only to fall into bankruptcy later when the business failed. She had taken on a loan as a guarantor of the business and had no money to repay the debts.

Without wanting to alarm her parents and with no money left, Amy went back home and started working at her family's business. Her parents had planned for her to eventually take over the helm of the company. One evening at a social dinner,

Amy met a man named Nab and they soon started dating. Nab was good with words and he knew how to gain Amy's trust. In a short time, Nab proposed marriage to Amy and she agreed despite the objection of her parents. Later they incorporated a business together and Nab named the company after Amy—Amy Investment Private Limited. Nab put Amy in charge as the owner of the company while he set up a subsidiary company. With the network of Amy's family, the business did well. Nab then got Amy to sign several checks and work orders that were later found out to be fraudulent.

Then Amy came home one evening and saw a note on her dining table that read, "I'm sorry, goodbye. Luv, Nab," and next to it was Nab's wedding ring.

III.   Pursue Wisdom

> *The crown of the wise is their riches.* —Proverbs 14:24, NKJV

> *Wisdom is a tree of life to those who embrace her; happy are those who hold her tightly.* —Proverbs 3:18, NLT

> *The life which is unexamined is not worth living.* —Socrates

Living free

Our words, acts, and decisions have impact on our lives and on the people around us. Even careless words, whether used consciously or unconsciously, may leave a taint on the hearts of those that hear them. Our decisions, likewise, have the effect of changing our lives for the better or the worse when actions are taken. Those decisions will send us into a place of blessings or a place of regret. Often where we end up is the result of a series of decisions that we have undertaken.

Having said that, it is possible to reroute a plan when a mistake is made. The mistake is not carved in stone until we continue to take the same mistaken route over and over, producing poor results, with no plan to reroute the course even though we know that it is the result of poor choices.

When we find ourselves in an undesirable position, instead of sinking into misery while thinking it is over, we should humbly ask God for wisdom and to lead us out of it. God in His mercy and grace will show us the path that we have fallen missed and lead us to where we should be.

Certainly it would be better if no unwise decision was made at the outset—if we wholly followed God and submitted to Him. Ask God to show you His plan and call for your life and to direct you towards it. The vision will show you the direction to focus on so that unwanted distractions cannot disrupt your course. Often when you do not have a focus, you become easy prey for scams and distractions as anything that seems interesting can easily pull you in.

Your focus gives you the strength to uncover the path that God has predetermined for you, and as you continue to walk in Him, the Holy Spirit will guide you from within. Any time there is a lack of peace while making a decision, simply step back and do not proceed, no matter how attractive the potential outcome seems. It is the Holy Spirit guiding you, for only God can see through the present into the future. Humans cannot. At times, when our sensors become blocked and we cannot sense the Holy Spirit leading, it is often due to the lust of our flesh that we desperately want a particular thing. The desperation we feel causes us to be blinded to the Spirit, and all our mind can think about is how to attain that thing.

Only when we decide to let go of our human flesh and the urge to possess is our spiritual sensor turned back on to lead us in the right direction. Desperation will always hide the truth from us and show us only what we want to see, and we will become vulnerable, deceived into acting in a way that is less than God's best for us. The devil knows what will arouse our desire and will present that thing in such a way that it will capture our heart. Only by submitting to God can we break away from the devil's trap.

God's plan for us will always see us progressing into a higher place, and it is only by His grace and not through our effort. When we let go of our desire to have something and wholly commit our lives to God's will, His grace will unfold to us over time and we will end up having it better than we originally wanted. This applies to everything in life—material things, careers, money, relationships, marriage, and childbearing.

Always remember that when God blesses us, there is no

sorrow added to it (Proverbs 10:22). The devil's plot, however, will give you unrest just when you think you have gotten what you wanted.

The mind governed by the flesh is death, but the mind governed by the Spirit is life and peace. —Romans 8:6, NIV

With wisdom we position ourselves to be blessed, gaining the favor of God and man. Our human knowledge can only show us as much as we can see with our eyes in the natural realm, but God's wisdom gives us an insight beyond that of human intellect.

Daniel in the Bible was one good example of a person to whom God gave great wisdom to see into visions and dreams. When the king was troubled by his dream and needed to have it interpreted, all the wise men in the palace were summoned to him but none of them were able to tell of the dream and its interpretation. Just about when the king wanted to have them all beheaded, Daniel came to him and requested some time to seek God so as to provide the king with an accurate interpretation. The king agreed. Daniel then went to the Lord, knelt before Him, and humbly asked for His help. He asked the Lord to show him the dream and its interpretation, and God did as Daniel asked. Not only were the wise men's lives saved as a result, Daniel was promoted to reign over them. When a new king took over the throne, Daniel continued to sit on favored ground. As Daniel's focus was on God and not man, he became extremely successful (Daniel 6:28).

When we let go and wholly submit to God, our lives become free. Free from the noises, the unrest, and the need to compare ourselves to the rest of society, and free to become true to ourselves and who God has made us to be. We dare to live out our call, knowing that God has our back. While an earthly, wealthy father can help his daughter to gain a foothold in her pursuit, he cannot protect her from the devil's plots. Only God, our heavenly Father, can watch over us all day long and guide us to safety. Even when we have no connections, no resources, and no skills to speak of, if it's a call from Him, He will equip us, orchestrate people, and clear our path, supernaturally opening doors for us. We do not have to manipulate things or people to give us favor; neither do we have to compromise on our values. No, when we follow God, He will make straight all the crooked paths for us (Proverbs 3:5–6).

> *Do not forsake wisdom, and she will protect you; love her, and she will watch over you.* —Proverbs 4:6, NIV

In Father God's perfect love

"And all that is mine is yours" (Luke 15:31, ESV). God has given us all things, and as we continue to walk in His love for us, trusting in Him, we will see the manifestation of our fruits and blessings take place at the right time. He is a good God who loves us perfectly, and not one of His people will be left alone without His care, for He would leave the ninety-nine sheep just for the one sheep that was lost (Luke 15:4, Matthew 18:12). His love for us is perfect. We can have faith to rest in Him and receive His love.

When we are conscious of God our heavenly Father's perfect love for us, we become free and live secure. His love does not waver, and how much He loves Jesus our Lord that is how much He loves us (John 17:23). We can come boldly to ask things from Him, trusting Him to work everything out for our good.

If an earthly father would give the best to his children, gifts that are often conditional, how much more would our heavenly Father give to us, lavishly and unconditionally. He would not give you a man, a job, a ministry, a project, or anything that is not a desire of your heart, and He would certainly not ask you to accept anything that will make you suffer. When He gives you something, He has already planted the desire for that thing in your heart, and it delights Him to see you enjoying it and to flourishing with it.

Take time to listen to Him. If a situation is constantly causing you distress, it is a sign that something has to change.

Sometimes the distress can be caused by a shift that seemed okay at first but that now has become a daily frustration. There could be several reasons for the distress—you could have outgrown the role that you were operating from or God may have another plan for you. Life is never linear, but we should always seek God and be ready to maneuver and flow with Him. If it's of God, you will feel the peace to move.

As blood and flesh imperfect beings living in an imperfect world, we are constantly being bombarded by the occurrences and negative voices around us. We are not quite stable with our emotions that go up and down even as we try to be still. It is therefore vital that we constantly remind ourselves of our true identity in Christ and that who we are is not conditional on any forces but the eternal words and promises of Father God alone.

When fear and anxiety creeps in, it is a sign that we do not have full confidence in the Father's love for us. We start to fall short in our behavior, and we start to push things out using our own effort, which leaves us feeling all bashed up and not getting the results that we want.

Only when we become conscious of Father God's perfect love for us can we rest easy, knowing that He is in control of all things and He will take care of us even when the situation looks unfavorable. We can trust Him to turn things around to our benefit. "Sit still, my daughter, until you know how the matter will turn out; for the man will not rest until he has concluded the matter this day" (Ruth 3:18, NKJV). When we rest in His love, He fights our battles for us in order to bring about successful outcomes. He promised that He would make our enemies our footstool (Psalm 110:1) as we rest in Him.

Father God will always come to our level to pick us up when we fail and to love us to wholeness if we allow Him. No approval is required, and we certainly do not need to prove ourselves just to receive from Him. Just come as you are and receive. Once you have tasted His grace, you will want to live right to glorify Him. You'll begin to have the desire to pursue goals that are birthed neither of emptiness nor fleshly need but out of the abundance that the Father has filled you with. The goals will fit with your persona and your gifts, and you will enjoy them without toil. This is the Father's love for you, His way to promote you to a higher height and to transform you from the inside out as you walk in your true identity in Christ.

When a child does not know the love of her father, she will often feel insecure, constantly needing validation from people, and she will have the urge to possess material things just to make herself feel good. She will hunger for love and look for it in all the wrong places, only to feel emptier afterwards and hanker for more. The woman at the well in John 4:13–14 was constantly pursuing men's love and that resulted in her having had five husbands and then the one she was staying with who was not her husband. Jesus told her to drink from His water so that she would not be thirsty again, implying that her thirst for men's love was an internal issue and the only way to quench it was to receive the living water from God so that she would forever be filled, and that living water is God Himself.

Only in the Father's love are we quenched. No earthly pursuit or man can fill us. When we are full on the inside, the abundance will overflow to our work and the people that God has put in our lives for us to enjoy. You can give love only when you have first received love from your Father. Your environment will begin to change for the better as you continue to draw from Him. The overflowing of His love will rub off in everything that you do, manifesting His grace through you.

Daughter, know that your Father God loves you very much. And in Him there is no fear, only perfect love (1 John 4:18). It is the Father's good pleasure to give you your heart's desire. He knows what you need and what is good for you, and His desire is for you to have life and life of abundance (John 10:10). Therefore be restful in Him and do not be shaken or give into temptation. The ways of evil are easy but it will only end up in misery. Do not pursue man but let man pursue you as you pursue God. Be patient and wait for the right one, your very own Boaz (depicted in the Bible as husband material) whom God has ordained for you.

For if you live according to the flesh, you will die; but if by the Spirit you put to death the misdeeds of the body, you will live. —Romans 8:13, NIV

Some precious ladies, after experiencing failed relationships, reacted in haste and began to distrust God, instead relying on their own effort to settle for men who were less than God's best for them. They were afraid of losing out and so they compromised, and this resulted in their lives being shortchanged.

"Who you marry, which is the ultimate partnership, is enormously important in determining the happiness in your life and your success," said Berkshire Hathaway CEO Warren Buffett in an October 2, 2017, interview on CNBC. His claim was supported by scientific research done by Carnegie Mellon University that showed that people with supportive spouses are more willing to take on big challenges and have also experienced greater growth and happiness in their lives.

If you are conscious of the Father's love for you, how could you not think that He would give you the best, someone that is the desire of your heart? The devil is capable of twisting the truth and making you think otherwise, and if you fall for his lies, life becomes a daily frustration. Though for some it might take a while for the right one to appear, trust God for He knows what He is doing and at the right time and the right place it shall come to pass.

No time is wasted while you are waiting for the Lord. In your wait, He is preparing you to become whom you were meant to be so that you fit nicely into His awesome plan for you, and that includes your Boaz. Just follow His lead and enjoy your journey, focusing on the Lord. You are unique and very precious, my daughter. No matter how long the wait, He will preserve your youth and renew your strength like an eagle (Isaiah 40:31) if you will wait on Him.

Have faith and patience and do not allow desperation to deceive you into believing that a frog is a prince. Frogs are aplenty, and when you are not careful and join in intimacy, they will croak you out of your blessings. The mind and heart become cluttered by the bondage formed through bodily connection, and breaking away becomes difficult.

If there is doubt, marriage should not proceed. Trust the Holy Spirit who has given you the discretion and discernment to know. Seek God and ask for His wisdom to guide you, and do not be swayed by the external voices around you. Marriage is a life covenant partnership in which two shall walk together till the end of life, thus it should not be entered into hastily. Neither have a relationship formed without marriage, as it will only lead to misery. Nothing is more beautiful to see than an anointed man and woman joined together through a marriage covenant, in which the husband is to love his wife just as Christ loved the church and gave Himself for her (Ephesians 5:25). This is a picture of what your destined Boaz should be like, my daughter.

In the book of Ruth, the evergreen beautiful love story, Boaz was shown as a generous gentleman. He was kind, gracious in his words, and put Ruth's interests before his own even before she became his wife. Though he was wealthy, he was humble and treated others with respect. He was open and transparent in his conduct, bold, and he took initiative, acting with purpose to do what he knew he ought to do, which in the context was to redeem Ruth. He did as he said he would, and he honored Ruth and took her as his wife. Boaz is an exemplar of the husband material that all daughters of God should look for in a man. He was also depicted as a model of Christ Jesus our Lord.

If you have faith to wait for your destined one, you will be richly rewarded in way that far exceeds your expectations, and certainly beyond anything that human effort can produce. God is faithful in His promises. When your Boaz appears, you will be ready to receive him, and together as a covenant pair you will perform mighty works of God to His glory, which is all a part of His plan for us. And through His plan your very own beautiful love story will be unveiled.

> *The Lord is good to those who wait for Him, to the soul who seeks Him.* —Lamentations 3:25, NKJV

IV.   Majority is not always right

> *Two roads diverged in a wood, and I, I took the one less traveled by, And that has made all the difference.* —Robert Frost

In business law, discharge is based on the majority rule principle on which business decisions are made. Minority shareholders are given the right to petition against decisions that are made in consideration of the fact that the majority is not always right.

The majority is not always right, yet people would rather conform to the popular ideas than act on their own beliefs, which then makes them part of the majority. They feel safe even if the majority is wrong. The fear of being different has somehow amputated their sense of what is right due to their lack of conviction and courage. Following the majority is easy, but it is rare that any breakthrough can be seen in these individuals' lives, as they mostly end up feeling empty and depressed.

All of us were created differently, with different personalities, gifts, and calls in life. We were made to live harmoniously with one another, but each of us has something that others

DAUGHTER, YOU'RE MEANT TO BE YOU

do not possess and so we can contribute to one another and benefit from each other. So when we try to be the same as others without following our own convictions, that is as good as disowning our fundamental selves. You are uniquely yours, my daughter, and you follow God's words and His leading. There is no need for you to compare yourself with others or to try to be like them. You walk by the Holy Spirit and He will guide you along the way.

When it's time to speak up, you speak up, and when it's time to act, you do so according to the Spirit's leading. People who can't accept you also can't accept the Holy Spirit in you, so be cool and shake them off, and God will get you new friends who will celebrate you.

During the time when Jesus was persecuted, no one stood up for Him, including those who had received His blessings. Because of their fear of being ostracized by the Pharisees, the people voted for Jesus to be exterminated and we do not hear about these people in the Bible anymore. When the majority ten spies at Kadesh Barnea spoke against going into the land that God had promised them, the people believed them and paid the price for it. They spent forty years wandering in the wilderness before dying without ever entering the Promised Land. Only Joshua and Caleb, the two spies who wholly believed God and spoke about how they would be able to take the land, made it into the Promised Land and thus enjoyed the land that was flowing with milk and honey. Both lived long and good lives. Caleb, in his old age at eighty-five, said that he was as strong as the day when Moses had sent him because he believed God. For that, God complimented Caleb as having a different spirit and therefore he was able to enter the Promised Land.

Likewise, God wants you, my daughter, to have a different spirit—a spirit of bold faith to believe. Conscientiously learn to close your ears to the voices of the naysayers that oppose your belief of what God has put in your heart to do.

Do not be intimidated by them but guard your heart with all diligence. You do not need approval from people for your security, as that is found in God alone. Life is too short to be around people who put you down and do not contribute to your growth. Be aware that they are simply projecting their own insecurities by dumping on you. Have the grace to walk away and receive none of their trash.

Though often the journey may be lonely and there will be times of doubt, continue to seek God and immerse yourself into His promises, prayer, and worship. Allow Him to sanctify your mind and show you more and more of Himself, for in His light you will see light. Trust Him to open new doors, and in due season you shall reap (Galatians 6:9–10).

> *You shall not follow a crowd to do evil.* —Exodus 23:2, NKJV

Minority rule

> *If you set out to be liked, you would be prepared to compromise on anything at any time, and you would achieve nothing.* —Margaret Thatcher

The minority here applies to those who live authentically by making unpopular choices, but choices that benefit others and themselves. These are people who live intentionally and by choice. Based on research studies, people who feel happy and satisfied with their lives are those who have set goals that are related to the welfare of others and have achieved them. This group formed only about ten percent of the population in the United States at the time when the research was carried out, and this group was also composed of people who had gained financial success.

Margaret Thatcher, the former prime minister of the United Kingdom, a.k.a. the Iron Lady, was the longest-serving British prime minister of the twentieth century, as well as the first woman to have held the office. She was known to be a strongheaded leader and someone who acted relentlessly and uncompromisingly in line with her principles, a powerful figurehead who influenced the nation in many ways. To celebrate their 70th anniversary in 2016, the BBC Radio programme *Women's Hours* voted Thatcher the most influential woman of the last seventy years. It was uncommon for women in her time to enter politics, much less to rule a country, yet she had exhibited a tremendous strength that put men to shame. During one of her interviews, she was asked if she received any concession from men of the opposing party, and her reply to the question was amazingly astonishing. "Why should they?" Thatcher exclaimed. "I wouldn't give them concession just because they are men!" (BBC, January 12, 1990). While Thatcher had her fair share of critics of the rigid policies that she implemented, there were many others who applauded her for her strength and courage to stand firm in her beliefs. Thatcher's influence revolutionized how women think about themselves, instilling strength of character in them, and at the same time transformed the way men think about women. While it would have been easier for her if she would have given into popular views, she made the tough call to stand firm in what she believed, which won her great honor.

Queen Elizabeth I was one of the longest-ruling queens in England's history besides Queen Victoria and Queen Elizabeth II, and she was the only queen who was never married but remained single all her life, which was unheard-of for women in the sixteenth century. Though she had many potential royal matches, suitors who asked for her hand in marriage, she was not interested. Having seen the challenges rulers faced because of royal marriages in the lives of her father and half-sister Mary I, she made the decision to remain single because she did not want to risk having someone else usurp her power and control over the political state of her country. She held her duty to her country in higher regard than her own personal affairs. Throughout her reign, Elizabeth's act of love for her country won her trust from the people. In her final years, Elizabeth spoke of "all my husbands, my good people" ("Elizabeth I," Wikipedia), suggesting that she was married to her kingdom and her subjects, to whom she stayed true till her death.

Before Rosa Parks, there was Ida B. Wells, who stood her ground on a train when she was asked to move to the smoking carriage that was reserved for black people. Wells was born into slavery in the nineteenth century, and she was part of the first generation of African Americans freed from slavery when the emancipation was proclaimed. Though slavery was lifted, the African Americans were still treated as lower-class citizens by society. Public transportation and public places were highly segregated, and African Americans were often unfairly treated. Wells decided when she was young that she was not going to tolerate the injustice but instead fight for herself and the rights of her community. When the conductor tried to drag her out of her seat, Wells bit his hand, but she was still forcefully dragged out by three other men. Wells then sued the railway company and won the case, but the verdict was later overturned somehow. Though she was greatly disappointed by the huge injustice and the situation in the country, she never gave up in fighting for her rights. She went on to become a journalist and wrote about the many cases of brutal injustice that had happened to her community. She also held campaigns for women's suffrage, and she formed several organizations that backed her causes. Though Wells died thirty-seven years before the Civil Rights Act was enacted in 1968—the act that ended segregation and discrimination against race, color, religion, and gender in the United States—what Wells had done throughout her life, her legacy, had unquestionably contributed to the enactment of the legislation.

I have learned over the years that when one's mind is made up, this diminishes fear; knowing what must be done does away with fear. —Rosa Parks

An Indian woman who worked at a film-processing factory, Grunwick, finally had enough of the unfair treatment she had received from her employer, gathered a group of one hundred women, and walked out of the factory with them in protest. The woman's name was Jayaben Desai. She was born in Gujarat, India, but she moved to East Africa and then finally settled in Britain with her husband and children as permanent residents. Life in Britain was not easy for immigrants and they often had difficulty finding jobs. Desai first worked as a seamstress while taking care of her children, and when her children had grown up she took up a job at the Grunwick factory. Many of the employees at the factory were South Asian immigrant women like herself. As these women were often desperate for work in order to make ends meet, they would accept almost anything so long as they got a job. That gave the employer the opportunity to exploit them, offering them a low pay rate and deplorable working conditions. The women's dissatisfaction, however, persuaded them to join Desai in the strike against Grunwick, and they went to more than a thousand workplaces all across Britain to garner support. By the summer of the following year, twenty thousand people had joined them in picketing the factory. Unfortunately, they were defeated and many were arrested, and the boss at Grunwick still would not budge and refused to accept their demands. It was, however, not all a lost cause; Grunwick did provide the remaining workers at the factory a better deal after the strike. At the same time, due to the huge impact of Desai and her strikers, workplaces around Britain improved as a result.

A learned Chinese woman born to an upper-class family in the nineteenth century sailed to Japan solo and left behind her family with the intent to carve out a new identity for herself as a warrior woman. Qiu Jin, having experienced terror and damages during the Boxer Rebellion uprising, as well as the oppressive behavior of her husband, left her hometown in pursuit of her interest and came back again some years later. Qiu was at the forefront of an emerging wave of new feminists who believed in women's rights and the equal treatment of men and women. She detested the cultural expectations that women were to stay at home, bind their feet, and accept arranged marriages. During her time in Japan, she joined revolutionary groups and enrolled herself in rigorous physical education classes that included sword fighting and bomb making. She then returned to China with the purposes of advancing women's causes and toppling the Qing patriarchal rule. She founded the *Chinese Women's Journal*, a publication that encouraged women to have independent income and be educated, and to emancipate themselves from the hands of men. She then plotted her revolution by educating the young on military skills and assassination of Qing officials. Unfortunately, her plans were discovered and, with no mercy, Qiu was captured and beheaded at the age of thirty-one. Before her death, she wrote a letter to a friend stating her determination to die for the revolutionary cause. In a way, Qiu's death was not a surprise to herself but a decision that she had made the day she chose to embark on her pursuit. She was prepared to die for her cause.

These women, whose lives were driven by a sense of purpose, knew that life had to be better than what they were familiar with. They were leaders who took responsibility and did what was right for themselves and their people. Though their lives were far from easy, their determination had their minds made up.

While these examples were mostly of women whose legacies contributed to world revolutions, having an impact does not necessarily require an upheaval. Instead, it can be speaking up when you have something to share, a story to inspire; it can also be the courage to stand up for the weak or for a project or a cause that you believe in, making a contribution to the greater good. No matter what it is that you plan to do, always be led by the Holy Spirit who dwells within you and will guide you in all truth and safety.

Be Original

> *The woman who follows the crowd will usually go no further than the crowd. The woman who walks alone is likely to find herself in places no one has been before.* —Albert Einstein

> *Whenever you find yourself on the side of the majority, it is time to pause and reflect.* —Mark Twain

> *One man with courage makes a majority.* —Andrew Jackson

Proverbs 14:1 says "the wise woman builds her house, but with her own hands the foolish one tears hers down" (NIV). The house here signifies your life and all of your faculties—the state of your mind, your heart, your choices, and all that you do.

The diligence to constantly seek the Lord, walking in His way and trusting in Him, is the cornerstone of wisdom that will build up our lives. Wisdom is personified as a female in the Bible, hence I believe it's a gift that was first given to daughters of God. That makes wisdom a natural attribute that women possess and when they walk in it, its power is released. As a lady, you do not need to fight like a man does to get what you want, neither do you need to function like the people of the world who compromise their values just to get ahead. No, you just need the wisdom of God and He will guide you in your steps.

You will not trip if you follow wisdom and do not act in haste. When others act out of fear and settle for less, you are clear on your identity in Christ and take courage to walk away when your values are in danger of being compromised. Though you may be shaken when sudden terror strikes, know that nothing can harm you. Challenges may roar at you, but you can stand tall and bold in faith, trusting God and allowing His wisdom to guide you.

Maybe things have not turned out the way you wanted and the wait has been protracted. "It's been too long, it's overdue!" you cry. You look at the sinners around you and they seem to have a good life; you cannot understand this and are tempted to follow their ways. Don't be deceived, my daughter, these were lies and lies will not sustain. The day will come and the truth shall be shown, and the lies will be no more. The temporal joy will be turned by the darkness into lifelong grief when the light comes in. Jesus is the light, and only by following the light will you see light, and the righteous (you!) shall shine brighter and brighter until the perfect day (Proverbs 4:18–22). This is His promise for you. Hold on to it. He will not fail.

You are righteous in His eyes. Keep your focus on God and what He has put in your heart, and be led by the Spirit to act out in faith. In time you shall see the manifestation of all the blessings that He has prepared for you.

Certainly this is not for the majority but for His children who would follow Him. Trust not what you see, feel, and touch but instead trust in God alone and His promises for you. He will resolve all your misfortune and the challenges that you are experiencing, and He will make your enemies your footstool. You will come out glorified, having much more than before, beautiful things that you did not create (Deuteronomy 6:10–11).

And be not conformed to this world: but be ye transformed by the renewing of your mind, that ye may prove what is that good, and acceptable, and perfect, will of God. —Romans 12:2, KJV

Be yourself; everyone else is already taken. —Oscar Wilde

Be original by not following the hypes and others around you but instead being who you were made to be and running your own race with what God has given you, and you will be successful. Comparison is unnecessary as each person has a different call. Looking at what others are doing will only distract you and pull you in the wrong directions, resulting in wasted resources.

People who are successful in life do not usually adhere to the common way. Fred Smith, an American billionaire and the founder of FedEx, is a good example of a person who had a unique mind of his own and who became greatly successful as he innovated his beliefs into his product. Smith started the company based on a concept of overnight delivery. When he wrote the idea in his college thesis, his professor felt that it was not practical and graded him poorly, giving him only a marginal score. Smith did not give up on his idea, however, and several years later he founded the world's first overnight delivery company, changing the transportation industry forever.

In John 21:21–22, Peter asked Jesus about His plan for John, and Jesus replied by saying, "What is that to you? You follow Me" (John 21:22, NKJV). Likewise, we are to follow Jesus and that is all we need to do. His grace will be there to see us through. You are God's precious daughter, and you were made to worship and glorify Him by living the victorious life that He planned for you. This is who you are and where you should be.

The majority in the world is mostly made up of the average lot who have no clarity of what they want in life, so they will always follow to the easiest path and tread just enough to survive. On the contrary, the originals who dare to follow their call are successful and able to rise up above. They do not like the idea of being common, and they would give up the opportunity to rise up the corporate ladder in order to pursue what God put in their hearts. Instead of looking for a husband to provide for them, original women look to God to supply. They are more concerned about their personal growth and soul's prosperity than about following the path of the majority.

Daniel 3 portrayed three faithful men of God, Shadrach, Meshach and Abednego, who declined the king's command to worship the idol statute that he had created for himself. By defying the order, they were thrown into the hot furnace to be burnt to death. A miracle happened and four men were seen walking in the furnace. The fourth was believed to be God, and all were unharmed. (When God is in our midst, all shall be well for us, His children). The king was amazed and asked for their release, and found out that not only their bodies were unharmed but their hair and robes were also intact with no smell of fire. The king knew then that it was God who had saved them, and he was impressed by their faithfulness and courage, so he had them promoted to rule over the province.

When everyone was paying homage to the villain, Mordecai stood by his faith to bow to no one except God, who promoted him to prevail over his enemies through divine interventions (Esther 8). When people of Jericho were greatly in fear, Rahab's faith and courage led her to negotiate with the spies and that saved her and her family while all others in the city were destroyed (Joshua 2–6). When women in ancient times were not entitled to inheritances from their fathers, the daughters of Zelophehad stood up and petitioned for their portions and received them (Numbers 27:1–11). When the people of Israel were fearful of the giant Goliath, the shepherd boy David was not intimidated. He challenged this threat and won credence with the people, who then supported him throughout his time as king of Israel (1 Samuel–2 Samuel). While the majority of the spies returned from the land of Canaan with bad reports, Caleb and Joshua believed in God's promises and came back with good news. This allowed them to enter and possess the land while the rest of their generation died without entering it (Numbers 14:30). The list goes on and on, but you get the point.

Yes, faith. Though you have faith, being an original will often cause you to be tested, but I beseech you to stay steadfast as you put your focus on God, and do not be deterred. The day when you decide to follow your call and run your own race, you should also disregard the need to be approved by others. The truth of the matter is that you will experience more people sneering at you than people cheering you on. The majority will always be the majority, and will act in the ways that the majority acts, so expect them to behave in that manner and you will not be disappointed. This will also help you to discern the right people to be your friends and to filter out the rest.

Do not believe anyone who tells you that your life should

be ordinary, for that is far from the truth. You are made to be exceptional and you have a call in life. The more topsy-turvy your path and the more setbacks you experience that are not of your choice, the more extraordinary your life will be. The days ahead have been made beautifully for you, and you have been prepared for them. Therefore, do not waste the talents and gifts that God has given to you. Instead, use them extensively and His grace will see you shine in life.

> Be original and true to yourself, my daughter. You are made to shine.

> *Let your light so shine before men, that they may see your good works and glorify your Father in heaven.* —Matthew 5:16, NKJV

> *But even if you should suffer for what is right, you are blessed. "Do not fear their threats; do not be frightened."* —1 Peter 3:14, NIV

THE AUTHOR

Yvonne Sophia Low is a passionate and constant learner and a believer in the grace of God through faith in Jesus Christ. Since the day she was born, treading through life has been anything but easy, with countless bumps and challenges and heartbreaks and pains that have never stopped trying to defeat her. Yet at the same time the fingerprints of God have been prevalent in her life and have been seen in the victories over every crisis she has faced. As a suicide survivor, she has firsthand experience of the love of God. It is this unconditional perfect love that has given her the faith to pursue and be satisfied with all her heart's desires.

This book, *Daughter, You're Meant to Be YOU,* begun in 2015, is inspired and led by the Lord. The message in the book has guided and benefitted Yvonne personally throughout the years, and by God's grace, each day she continues to learn from and lean on the Holy Spirit. It is Yvonne's prayer that through this book many precious souls will be touched and come to find peace and truth in living in God's love, having His grace to live life elegantly with purpose, and be led by the Holy Spirit in living out their lives full of His abundance and joy.

Yvonne is a child sponsor partnering with World Vision and is currently serving at New Creation Church in Singapore.

Visit https://daughteryouaremeanttobeyou.com.